T0005718

CICADA SYMPHONY

Sue Fliess

illustrated by
Gareth Lucas

Albert Whitman & Company
Chicago, Illinois

There's a secret you should know:
bugs are lurking down below.
In the earth, nymphs lay in wait
for their turn to...activate!

Young cicadas are
called nymphs. They
do not hibernate when
they are underground.
They feed on juice and
sap from tree roots.

There are about three
thousand species, or
kinds, of cicadas. Some
emerge, or come up from
the ground, every year.

Other cicadas emerge in large groups called broods after ten years or more. In the US, there are cicadas that emerge every thirteen or seventeen years.

Ground warms up. They're moving now.
Hundreds, millions, trillions, wow!
Time to molt: one, two, three, four.
Eager, ready to explore.

When the soil warms up, that's the signal for nymphs to dig. There can be hundreds of tiny emergence holes, sometimes called chimneys, where nymphs break through the soil's surface under trees.

Cicada nymphs change their skin four times before they reach the soil's surface.

When a cicada nymph molts, it breaks out of its hard outer skin, called an exoskeleton. Underneath is a soft skin that soon hardens. This change is called metamorphosis.

To the surface, up they go.
No one tells them. They just know.
Gripping tight for one last change.
Split. Pop! Wriggle. Looking strange.

Cicadas climb any standing object, like a tree or a post. As a cicada grips the object tightly, its exoskeleton splits up the back.

The adult cicada
wriggles out.

Plump cicada, milky-white,
gleams and glistens in the light.
Veins turn orange, soon complete.
Blue-black body. Clawlike feet.

A newly emerged adult
cicada looks almost alien.

In a few hours, the cicada grows
to full size. Its body hardens and
turns brown, black, bluish-black, or
bright colors. Adults can be as long
as your little finger. Veins in the
cicada's wings turn bright orange.

After their wings unfold and dry, the cicadas are adults. They grip tree bark with strong claws.

Two sets of eyes bulge and become bright red. One set sees light and dark. The other set sees the world around it.

Done expanding to full size,
watches with two sets of eyes.
Four large wings unfold and dry.
Climb to treetops, safe and high.

Rest on branches.
Suck in water.
Keeping cool
as days grow hotter.

Adults suck juice from trees and plants with long suction tubes to keep cool on hot summer days.

Flying fast, but crashing too.
Smacking into things...and you!
Not to worry, they don't bite
or pinch or sting or even fight.

After several days, adults can fly and call to each other. They crawl or fly high into the treetops.

Cicadas are clumsy but harmless.

Critters feast on them for lunch.
Protein with an extra crunch!

Birds, squirrels, chipmunks, raccoons, turtles, skunks, and dogs eat cicadas. In some parts of the world, people eat them too. There are too many cicadas for all of them to be eaten, and a great number of them go on to mate and lay even more eggs.

Males are known for one great thing:
not their looks, but how they sing!
A symphony of clicking starts.
They already know their parts.

Only males sing, or buzz, to call females and sometimes to keep other males away. They often stay close together in trees in "chorusing centers" that attract females. There can be 750,000 males in one acre.

Eeee-ooo! Eeee-ooo!
they drone on.
Then quiet down from dusk till dawn.

Cicadas have two special muscles in their abdomens that they tighten and loosen to make a clicking sound. They can do this more than three hundred times each second! Because a male cicada's abdomen is mostly hollow, the clicking sounds loud, like a drum.

Each cicada species has its own song.

Cicadas can be as noisy as a lawnmower, motorcycle, or chainsaw. The male cicada's ears don't hear while it calls, so that it doesn't deafen itself.

Males extend their invitations.
Females fly to their locations,
check out mates from tree to tree,
then flick their wings if they agree.

A female hears the males sing. She flicks her wings, making a clicking sound, to let one male know she accepts his invitation to mate.

Pregnant mamas choose a twig.
Slice it open. Dig, dig, dig!
Lay five hundred eggs or more.
Survival's what they're aiming for.

About three to five days after the female becomes pregnant, she lays her eggs. She slices or digs a line in a tree branch or twig with a saw-like part of her abdomen and lays her eggs there. One female can lay up to six hundred eggs.

Grown cicadas don't live long...
but keep their species going strong.

MOLT

NYMPH

Adult cicadas live for
about five weeks.

ADULT

EGGS

Dying once their work's complete,
now the cycle can repeat.
Eggs all hatch and new nymphs fall,
burrow, grow, begin to crawl...

Nymphs break out
of their eggs and
fall to the ground.

Scientists aren't sure how cicadas track the passage of time or "count the years," but think it's a combination of the ground warming and the nymphs detecting changes in the taste of tree root juices. Sometimes cicadas get it wrong and emerge too soon.

Hidden deep, it seems they're gone.
The world above them moving on.
Patient insects buried, still.
Counting years and years until...

The ground warms up, and that's their cue
to rise again...they always do.
They'll perform for you and me...
a grand cicada symphony!

Glossary

abdomen: The part of a cicada's body below the thorax.

acre: A unit of land equal to 43,560 square feet in the US. When cicada broods emerge, there may be as many as 750,000 cicadas in one acre.

antennae: Two short structures on a cicada's head that allow the cicada to smell and sense touch, temperature, and vibration.

molt: To shed hair, feathers, shells, horns, or an outer layer regularly. Cicadas molt many times, leaving their exoskeletons on the ground and on tree trunks.

protein: A material that occurs naturally in plants and animals. Cicadas are a great source of protein, which is why many animals prey on them.

thorax: The middle part of a cicada's body between the head and the abdomen.

tymbals: Membranes, or thin layers, in a male cicada's hollow abdomen. Males vibrate their tymbals to make a clicking sound that attracts females. Females also have tymbals, but these are outside their abdomens.

Author's Note

In 2021, my husband Kevin and I lived through Brood X, as this group of cicadas was called, in my state of Virginia. I found the buzzing sound thrilling and we witnessed each stage of the cicada lifecycle on our walks. We usually had our dogs with us. One of them ignored the insects and the other snacked on them! Occasionally we measured the volume of the cicadas' clicking, and once it registered at over ninety decibels! Kevin noticed my fascination with cicadas and encouraged me to write this book. I've dedicated this book to him.

Children's Reference Books

Leaf, Christina. *Cicadas*. Minneapolis: Bellwether Media, 2018.

Pringle, Laurence. *Cicadas!: Strange and Wonderful*. Honesdale, PA: Boyds Mills Press, 2010.

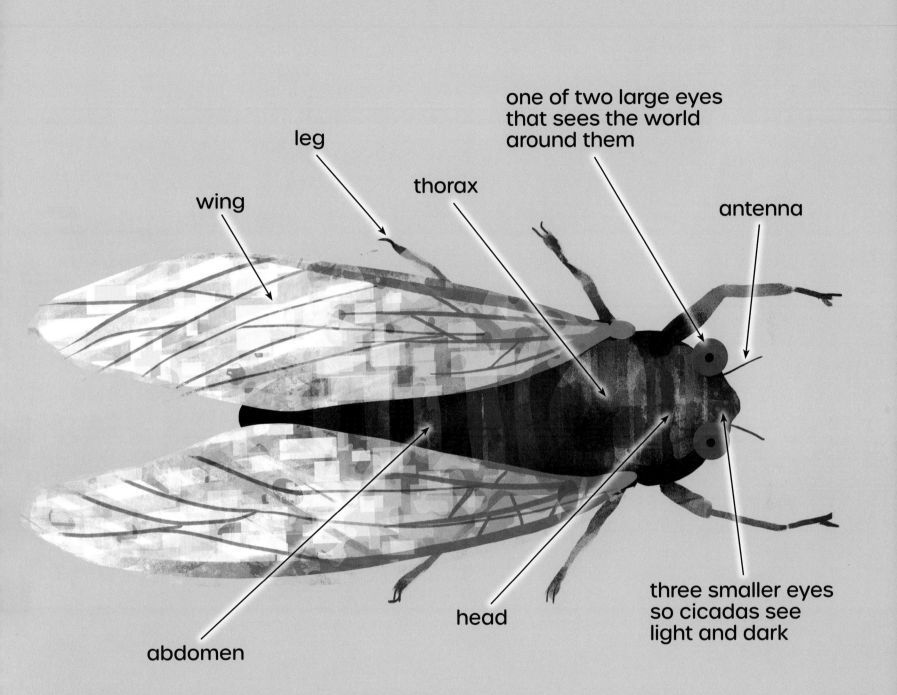

one of two large eyes that sees the world around them

leg

thorax

wing

antenna

abdomen

head

three smaller eyes so cicadas see light and dark

The average size of a cicada is 0.9—1.2 inches.

For Kevin, who makes everything "click"—SF

To my Brood V—GL

Library of Congress Cataloging-in-Publication data is on file with the publisher.
Text copyright © 2023 by Sue Fliess
Illustrations copyright © 2023 by Albert Whitman & Company
Illustrations by Gareth Lucas
First published in the United States of America in 2023 by Albert Whitman & Company

ISBN 978-0-8075-1161-9 (hardcover)
ISBN 978-0-8075-1162-6 (ebook)

All rights reserved. No part of this book may be reproduced or transmitted in any form
or by any means, electronic or mechanical, including photocopying, recording, or by any
information storage and retrieval system, without permission in writing from the publisher.

Printed in Canada
10 9 8 7 6 5 4 3 2 TCP 28 27 26 25 24

Design by Rick DeMonico

For more information about Albert Whitman & Company,
visit our website at www.albertwhitman.com.

FSC
www.fsc.org

MIX
Paper | Supporting
responsible forestry
FSC® C011825